SCHOLASTIC

GRADE 2

Success With Writing

AF647446

New York • Toronto • London • Auckland • Sydney
• New Delhi • Hong Kong

Teaching Resources

State Standards Correlations

To find out how this book helps you meet your state's standards, log on to **www.scholastic.com/ssw**

Written by Lisa Molengraft
Cover design by Ka-Yeon Kim-Li
Interior illustrations by Mark Mason
Interior design by Quack & Company

ISBN-13 978-93-5103-752-1

Reprinted by Scholastic India Pvt. Ltd., February 2015, November 2016, 2018, July 2025

Printed at Shivam Offset Press, New Delhi.

Introduction

One of the greatest challenges teachers and parents face is helping children develop independent writing skills. Each writing experience is unique and individualized, making it each child's responsibility to plan, expand, and proofread his or her work. However, the high-interest topics and engaging exercises in this book will both stimulate and encourage children as they develop the necessary skills to become independent writers. This book uses these strategies to introduce grade-appropriate skills that can be used in daily writing assignments such as journals, stories, and letters. Like a stepladder, this book will help children reach the next level of independent writing.

Table of Contents

Name ______________________________

You're Sharp!

A sentence begins with a **capital letter.**

Circle the words that show the correct way to begin each sentence.

many Of / Many of — my friends are in second grade.

Our teacher / our Teacher — keeps a fish tank in our classroom.

The reading / the reading — center has many good books.

the globe / The globe — helps us find places around the world.

we Study / We study — about the weather.

Our class / our Class — won the reading contest.

Name ______________________________

Stick With It

A sentence begins with a **capital letter**.

Write the beginning words correctly to make a sentence.

1. art class ______________________ begins at noon.

2. today we ______________________ are making clay pots.

3. first, we ______________________ form the clay into balls.

4. the next ______________________ step is to make a hole in the ball.

5. my teacher ______________________ dries the pots.

6. next week ______________________ we will paint the pots.

Name ______________________________

A Whale of a Sentence

A **telling sentence** *ends with a* **period** *(.).*

Rewrite the sentences using capital letters and periods.

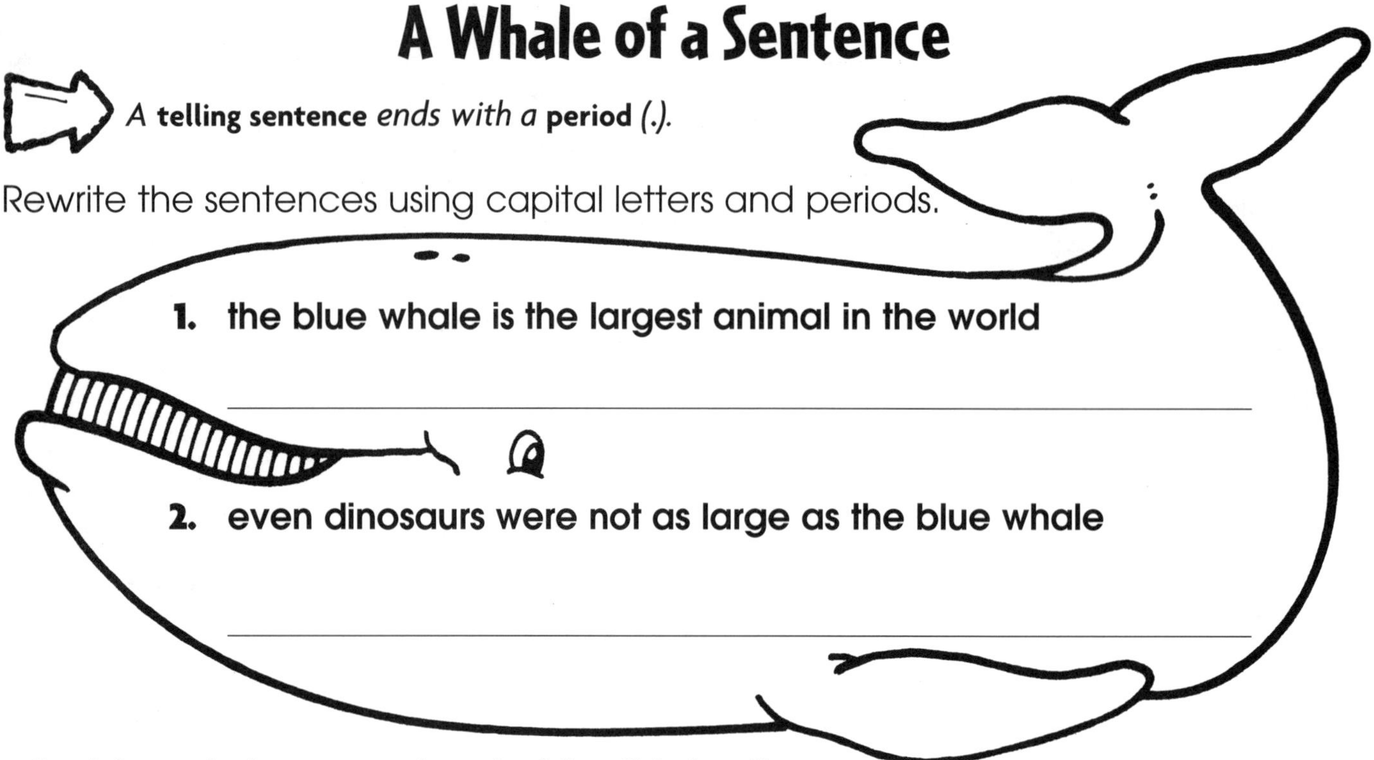

1. the blue whale is the largest animal in the world

____

2. even dinosaurs were not as large as the blue whale

____

3. blue whales are not part of the fish family

____

4. the blue whale has no teeth

____

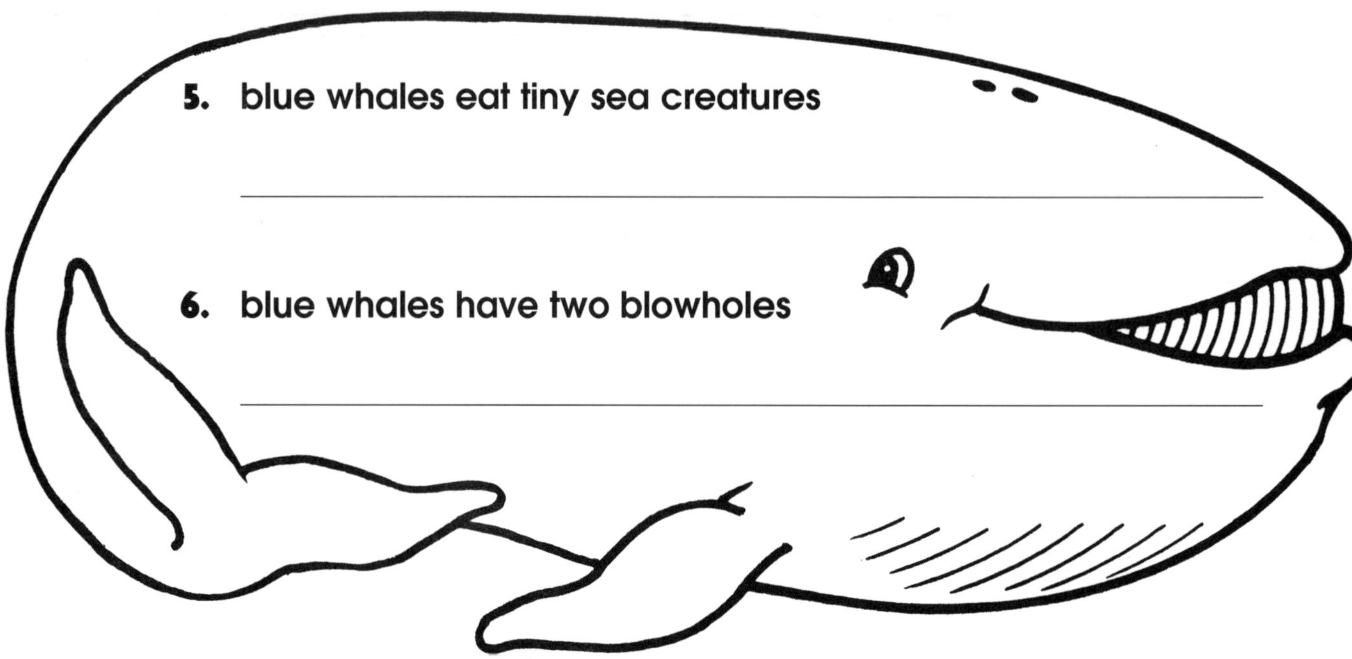

5. blue whales eat tiny sea creatures

____

6. blue whales have two blowholes

____

Name ______________________________ **Writing statements**

That Sounds Fishy to Me

A **telling sentence** *begins with a* **capital letter** *and ends with a* **period**.

Write a sentence about each fish. Remember to tell a complete idea.

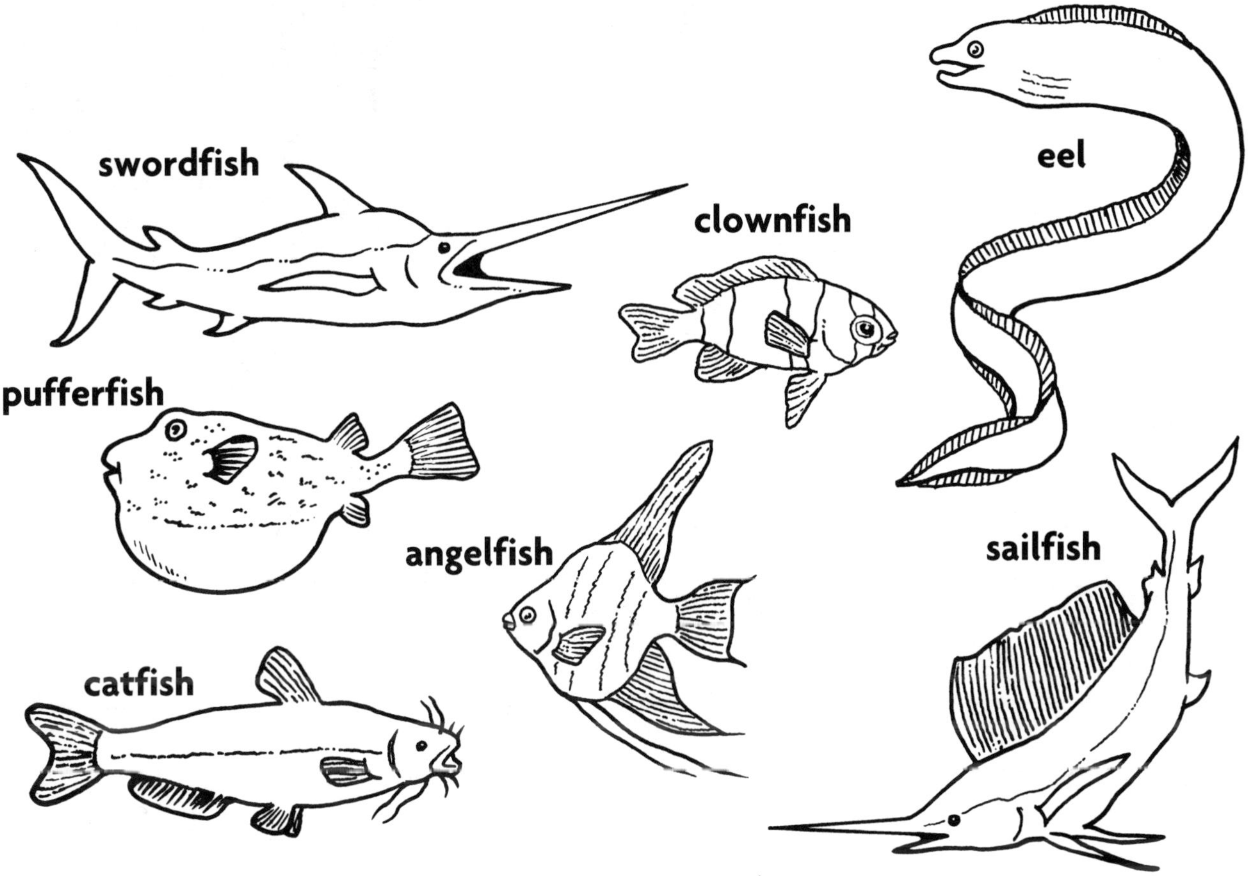

1. The swordfish has a long snout.
2. ______________________________
3. ______________________________
4. ______________________________
5. ______________________________
6. ______________________________
7. ______________________________

Ask Mother Goose

A sentence that asks a question ends with a **question mark** *(?). It often begins with one of these words.*

Who . . . *Where . . .* *Why . . .* *Could . . .*
What . . . *When . . .* *Will . . .*

Rewrite the questions using capital letters and question marks.

1. **where is the king's castle**

____

2. **who helped Humpty Dumpty**

____

3. **why did the cow jump over the moon**

____

4. **will the frog become a prince**

____

5. **could the three mice see**

____

Ask the Wolf

An **asking sentence** *begins with a* **capital letter** *and ends with a* **question mark (?)***.*
It often begins with one of these words.

How . . .	*Can . . .*	*Would . . .*
Did . . .	*Is . . .*	*Should . . .*

Imagine that you can meet the Big Bad Wolf. What questions would you ask him about Little Red Riding Hood and the Three Little Pigs? Use a different beginning word for each question you write.

1. How ______________________________
2. Did ______________________________
3. Can ______________________________

1. Is ______________________________
2. Should ______________________________
3. Would ______________________________

Pretend that you are the Big Bad Wolf. Write a sentence on another sheet of paper to answer each question above.

Is Your Head in the Clouds?

A **telling sentence** *ends with a* **period** *(.).*
An **asking sentence** *ends with a* **question mark** *(?).*

Finish each sentence by putting a period or a question mark in the cloud at the end.

1. Clouds can look like cotton balls, feathers, or blankets

2. Do you know what makes a cloud form in the sky

3. Have you ever seen dark clouds on rainy days

4. Dark clouds may bring thunderstorms

5. Can you imagine pictures in the clouds

6. White clouds drift across the blue sky

7. Why don't we see clouds every day

8. Rain, snow, sleet, and hail may fall from clouds

Find two telling sentences and two questions in one of your favorite books. Write them on another sheet of paper.

Name ______________________________

Sunny Se

Every sentence begins with a **capital letter**.
A **telling sentence** *ends with a* **period** *(.).*
An **asking sentence** *ends with a* **question mark** *(?).*

Rewrite each sentence correctly.

1. the sun is the closest star to Earth

____

2. the sun is not the brightest star

____

3. what is the temperature of the sun

____

4. the sun is a ball of hot gas

____

5. how large is the sun

____

6. will the sun ever burn out

____

On another sheet of paper, write a sentence with two mistakes. Ask a friend to circle the mistakes.

Name ______________________________

Camp Fiddlestick

A telling sentence is called a **statement**. *An asking sentence is called a* **question**. *Now ask yourself:*

How do sentences begin? How do statements end? How do questions end?

Write three statements and three questions about the picture.

Statements:

1. ______________________________

2. ______________________________

3. ______________________________

Questions:

1. ______________________________

2. ______________________________

3. ______________________________

Sing "Where is Thumbkin?" to yourself. Count the number of questions and statements in the song.

Name ______________________________

A Happy Camper

Complete:
Every sentence begins with a ____________________.
A statement ends with a ____________________.
A question ends with a ____________________.

Uh oh! Dalton was in a hurry when he wrote this letter. Help him find 10 mistakes. Circle them.

Dear Mom and Dad,

camp is so cool? today we went swimming? do you know what the best part of camp is. i think fishing is my favorite thing to do. did you feed my hamster. I really miss you?

Love,

Dalton

Now choose two questions and two statements from Dalton's letter. Rewrite each correctly.

1. ____

2. ____

3. ____

4. ____

On another sheet of paper, write a letter to a friend or family member. Include two statements and two questions.

Name ______________________________________

A Day at the Beach

A sentence that shows strong feeling or excitement is called an **exclamation.** *It ends with an* **exclamation point (!)**. *For example: Look at that shark!*

Finish each sentence by putting a period, a question mark, or an exclamation point in the shell at the end.

1. I wonder if Jamie will be at the beach today

2. Did you bring the beach ball

3. Look at the size of the waves

4. Where did I leave my sunglasses

5. Mom put snacks in the beach bag

6. Watch out for that jellyfish

7. Do you want to build a sandcastle

8. The sun is bright today

9. Did you see that sailboat

10. Don't step on that starfish

11. It is windy near the seashore

12. Should we put up an umbrella

Read these sentences: I see a sand crab. I see a sand crab! How does your voice change?

Seashore Sentences

Complete:

A ____________________ *ends with a period.*
A ____________________ *ends with a question mark.*
An ____________________ *ends with an exclamation point.*

Write a statement (S), a question (Q), and an exclamation (E) about each picture.

S ______________________________

____

Q ______________________________

____

E ______________________________

____

S ______________________________

____

Q ______________________________

____

E ______________________________

____

On another sheet of paper, write a statement, a question, and an exclamation about a cartoon in the newspaper.

Building Blocks

A good sentence has a part that tells who or what the sentence is about. This is called the **subject**.

Make a list of possible subjects to complete each sentence.

_____ jumped the fence.

1. ______________________

2. ______________________

3. ______________________

_____ is too full.

1. ______________________

2. ______________________

3. ______________________

A good sentence has a part that tells what happens. This is called the **action**.

Make a list of possible actions to complete each sentence.

We _____ on the playground.

1. ______________________

2. ______________________

3. ______________________

The cowboy _____ on his horse.

1. ______________________

2. ______________________

3. ______________________

On another sheet of paper, make a list of five subjects you would like to write about.

Keep Building!

Some sentences have a part that tells where or when the action is happening.

For each sentence, make a list of possible endings that tell where or when the action happens.

The wind blew ______________.

1. ______________
2. ______________
3. ______________

The baby tripped ______________.

1. ______________
2. ______________
3. ______________

Complete each sentence.

1. ______________________________ made us laugh last night.
2. The door leads ______________________________.
3. The crowd ______________________________ at the circus.
4. The paint bucket spilled ______________________________.
5. ______________________________ was never seen again.
6. The firefighter ______________________________ into the fire truck.

Get Your Ticket!

Write a sentence to match each picture. Be sure to include a subject, an action, and a part that tells where or when.

1. A boy climbs a tree in his backyard.

2. ____

3. ____

Find a cartoon in the newspaper. Use the pictures to write a sentence on another sheet of paper. Be sure to include a subject, an action, and a part that tells where or when.

Name ______________________

Slide Show

A sentence is more interesting when it includes a subject, an action, and a part that tells where or when.

Write three sentences and draw pictures to match.

subject	action	where or when

1. ______________________

subject	action	where or when

2. ______________________

subject	action	where or when

3. ______________________

Switch the sentence parts around to make three silly sentences! Write the sentences on another sheet of paper.

Name ______________________________

Mystery Bags

Describing words *help you imagine how something looks, feels, smells, sounds, or tastes.*

Make a list of words that describe the object in each bag below.

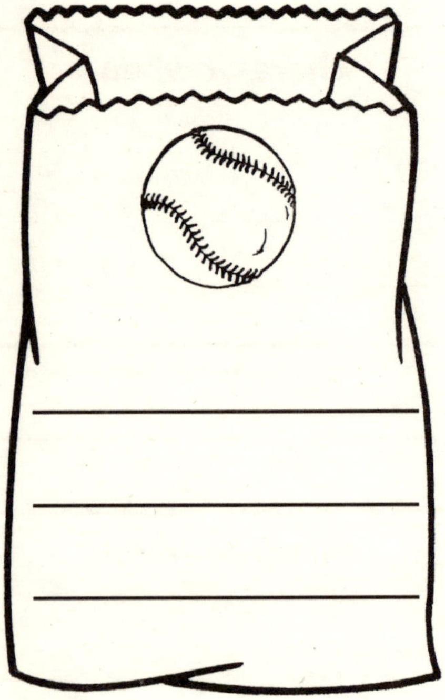

Use a paper sack to make a real mystery bag. Place an object in the bag and give describing clues to someone at home. Can he or she guess the mystery object?

Country Roads

A good sentence uses describing words to help the reader "paint a picture" in his or her mind.

Add a describing word from the list to finish each sentence.

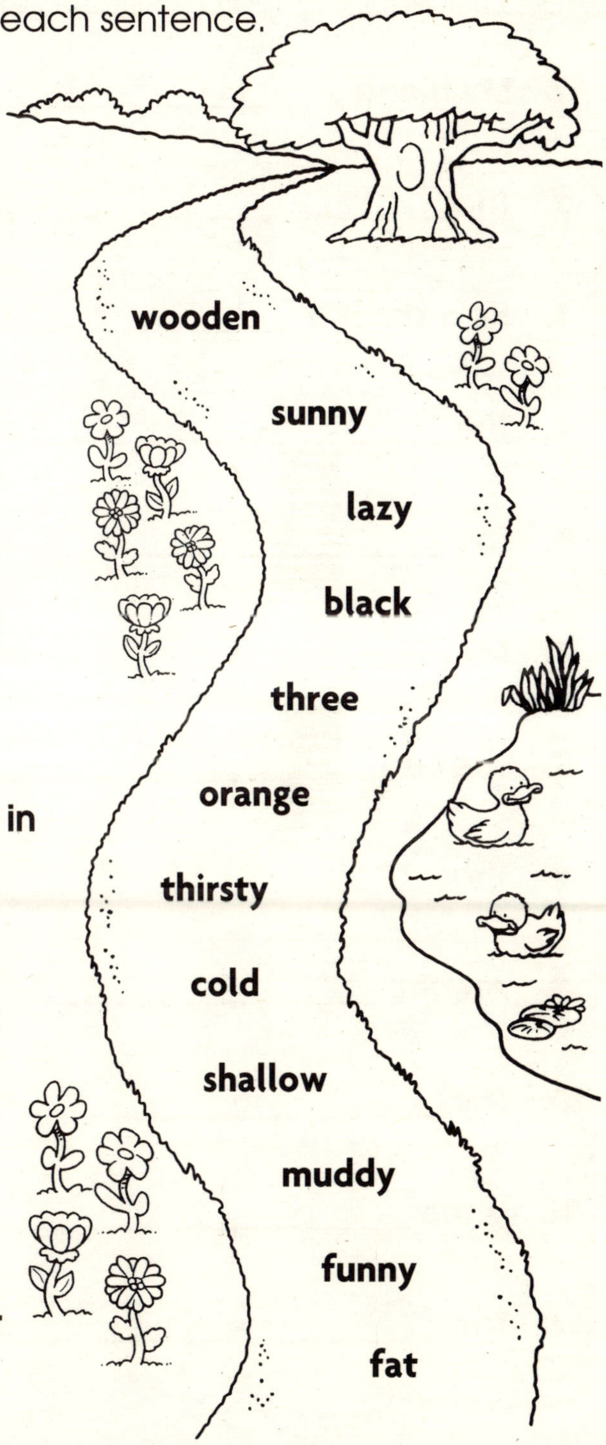

1. The ____________________ chicken laid ____________________ eggs in her nest.

2. The ____________________ barn keeps the ____________________ animals warm at night.

3. ____________________ carrots grow in the ____________________ garden.

4. Two ____________________ pigs sleep in the ____________________ pen.

5. The ____________________ cows drink from the ____________________ pond.

6. A ____________________ scarecrow frightens the ____________________ birds.

On another sheet of paper, write three sentences describing your favorite place to visit.

Name ________________________________

It's in the Bag

Describing words *make a sentence more interesting.*

Add a describing word to each sentence.

1. My friend's ____________________ dog has fleas!

2. The ____________________ popcorn is in the big bowl.

3. How did the ____________________ worm get on the sidewalk?

4. The ____________________ ocean waves crashed against the rocks.

5. The ____________________ ball broke a window at school!

6. My ____________________ skin itched from poison ivy.

7. The two ____________________ squirrels chased each other up the tree.

8. The ____________________sand felt good on my feet.

9. Are the ____________________ apples ready to be picked?

10. The ____________________ ball was hard to catch.

11. Is the ____________________ salamander hiding under the rock?

12. The ____________________ snow cone melted quickly.

Ask someone at home to make a mystery bag and give you clues about the object inside.

Name ______________________________

City Streets

A good sentence uses describing words.

Write a statement (S), a question (Q), and an exclamation (E) about the picture. Use each of the following describing words:

fast **busy** **crowded**

S ______________________________

____

Q ______________________________

____

E ______________________________

____

Describe a "mystery object" to a friend. Can he or she guess what you are describing?

Football Frenzy

A sentence is more interesting when it gives exact information.

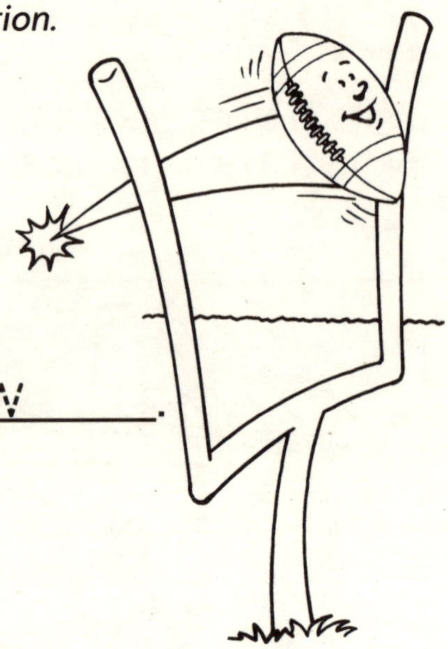

Replace each word to make the sentence more exact.

1. The **ball** game starts **soon**.

The soccer game starts now.

2. We are meeting **her** **there**.

We are meeting ______________ ______________.

3. Let's eat **this** and **that** before the game.

Let's eat ______________ and ______________ before the game.

4. I hope **they** score **some** points.

I hope ______________ score ______________ points.

5. **They** were also **there**.

______________ were also ______________.

6. **He** played a **good** game!

______________ played a ______________ game!

Name ____________________________________ **Expanding sentences**

Take Me Out to the Ball Game

A sentence is more interesting when it gives complete information.

Finish each sentence so that it answers the question.

1. **The players get to the stadium** **when.**

____

2. **The team is excited because** **why.**

____

3. **The fans arrive in** **what.**

____

4. **Flags are flying** **where.**

____

5. **A man sings the "Star-Spangled Banner"** **when.**

____

6. **The fans cheer for** **whom.**

____

7. **The ball is hit** **where.**

____

On another sheet of paper, write a sentence about your favorite game. Be sure to tell who plays the game with you.

Cake and Ice Cream

Two sentences that share the same subject can be combined to make one sentence by using the word and.

Rewrite the sentences by combining their endings.

1. **The party was fun.**
The party was exciting.

The party was fun and exciting.

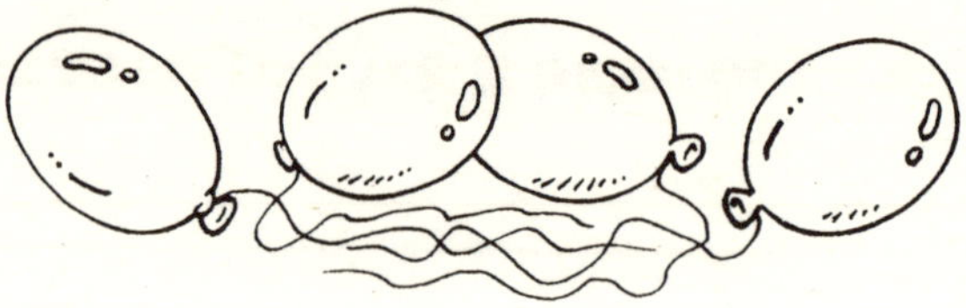

2. **We blew up orange balloons.**
We blew up red balloons.

____

3. **We ate cake.**
We ate ice cream.

____

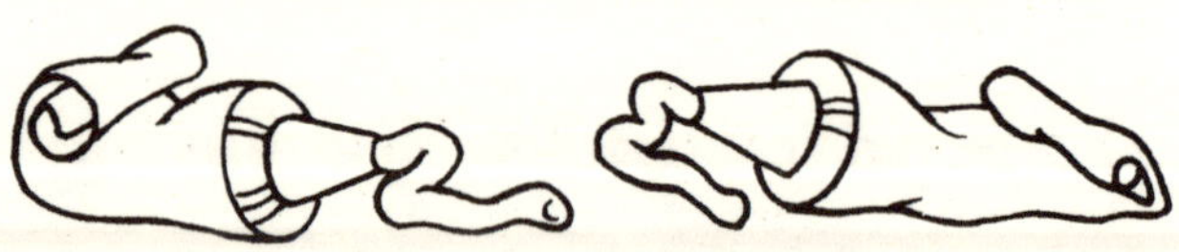

4. **The cake frosting was green.**
The cake frosting was yellow.

____

5. **We made a bookmark.**
We made a clay pot.

____

6. **We brought games.**
We brought prizes.

____

Name ______________________________ Combining sentences

Salt and Pepper

Two sentences that share the same ending can also be combined to make one sentence.

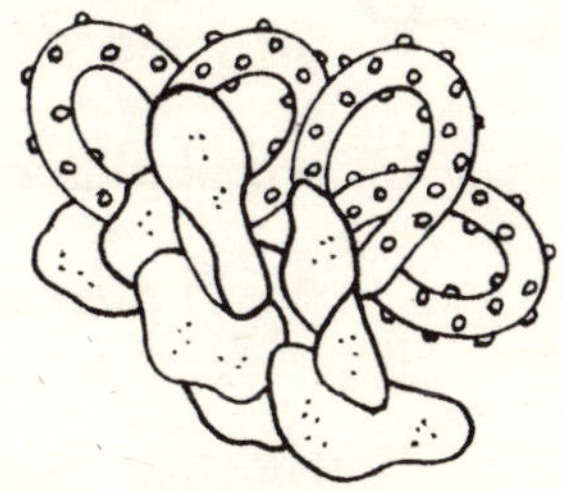

Rewrite the sentences by combining their subjects.

1. These peanuts are salty!
These pretzels are salty!

These peanuts and pretzels are salty!

2. The first graders eat lunch at noon.
The second graders eat lunch at noon.

____

3. Where is the salt?
Where is the pepper?

____

4. The napkins are on the table.
The forks are on the table.

____

5. Are the muffins in the oven?
Are the cookies in the oven?

____

6. Michael bought lunch today.
Stephen bought lunch today.

____

Great Gardening Tips

Sentences can also be combined to make them more interesting. Key words can help put two sentences together.

I will plan my garden. I am waiting for spring.

I will plan my garden while I am waiting for spring.

Combine the two sentences using the key word. Write a new sentence.

1. **Fill a cup with water. Add some flower seeds.** and

   ____

2. **This will soften the seeds. They are hard.** because

   ____

3. **Fill a cup with dirt. The seeds soak in water.** while

   ____

4. **Bury the seeds in the cup. The dirt covers them.** until

   ____

5. **Add water to the plant. Do not add too much.** but

   ____

6. **Set the cup in the sun. The plant will grow.** so

   ____

Name ____

Growing Sentences

Sentences can be combined to make them more interesting.

Write a combined sentence of your own. Use the given key word to help you.

1. while I watch TV while my mom makes lunch.

2. until ______________________________

3. because ______________________________

4. but ______________________________

5. or ______________________________

6. and ______________________________

On another sheet of paper, write a combined sentence of your own using one of these key words: ***after, before, during.***

Name ______________________________ Using commas in a series

The Sky's the Limit

Some sentences include a list. A **comma** *(,) is used to separate each item in the list.*

For example: Mrs. Jones asked the class to work on pages two, three, and four.

Fill in the blanks to make a list in each sentence. Watch for commas!

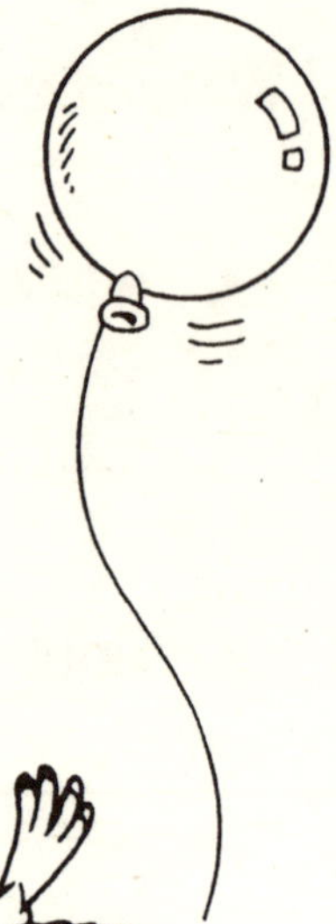

1. I ate ______________, ______________,

and ______________ for breakfast.

2. We stayed with Grandma on ______________,

______________, and ______________ nights.

3. I found ______________, ______________,

and ______________ in my party bag.

4. The boys played ______________,

______________, and ______________

at summer camp.

5. The ______________, ______________,

and ______________ ate the corn we scattered.

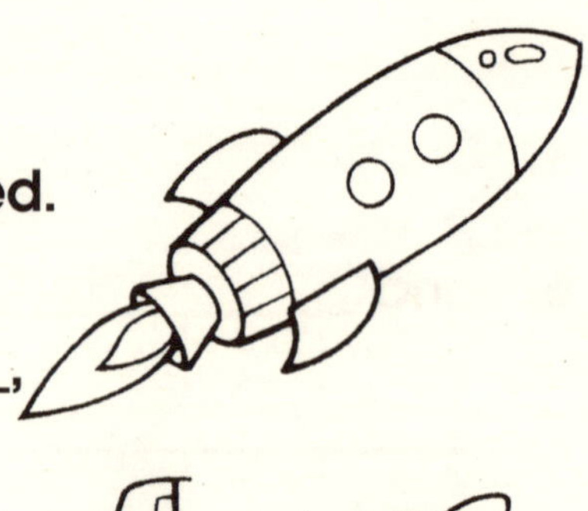

6. The pigs built their houses using ______________,

______________, and ______________.

Cut a balloon out of paper. On one side, list three objects that fly. On the other side, write a sentence that lists these objects.

Name ____________________

Up, Up, and Away

Some sentences include a list. A **comma** *(,) is used to separate each item in the list.*

Write a sentence that includes a list of the words that are given.

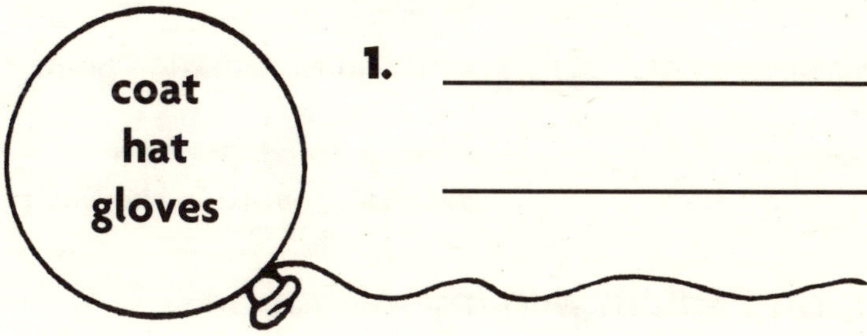

1. ____________________

____

2. ____________________

____

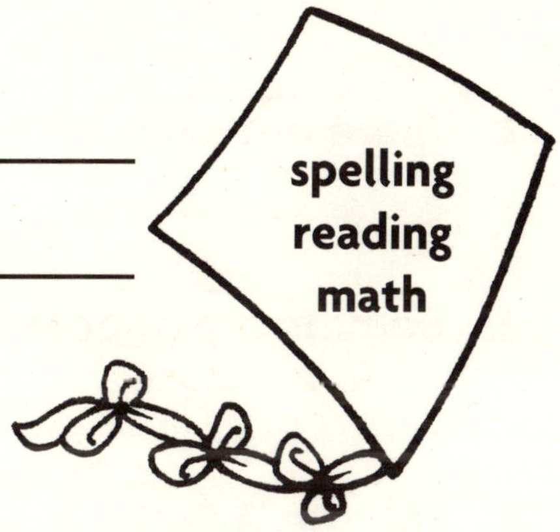

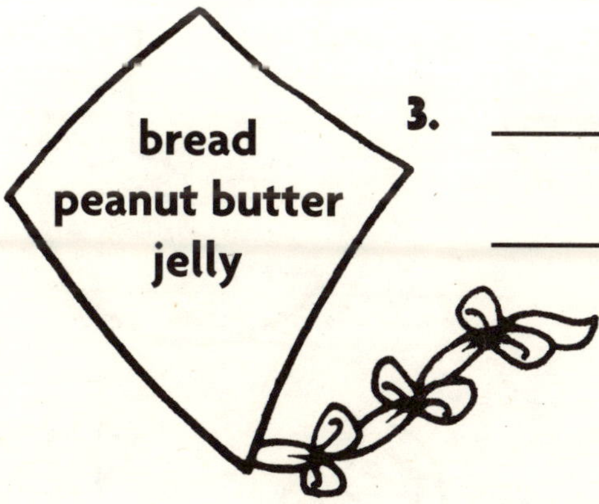

3. ____________________

____

4. ____________________

____

On another sheet of paper, write a sentence that lists colors or shapes of balloons.

Name ____________________ **Proofreading**

Out of This World

After you write a sentence, go back and look for mistakes. This is called **proofreading** *your work.*

Use the proofreading marks to correct the two mistakes in each sentence.

mars (≡ under m) = **Make a capital letter.**	(?) = **Add a question mark.**	(!) = **Add an exclamation point.**
(.) = **Add a period.**	(,) = **Add a comma.**	[ ] = **Add a word. (Write a describing word in the box.)**

1. Sometimes I can see mars Jupiter, and Saturn with my telescope.

2. There are ^ stars in our galaxy

3. comets are ^ pieces of ice and rock.

4. The sun is really a ^ star

5. is there life on any other planet

6. Look at that ^ shooting star

7. can you imagine traveling in space

8. i think I saw a ^ alien.

On another sheet of paper, write two sentences about space with two mistakes in each. Ask someone at home to proofread your sentences. Is he or she correct?

Smart About Saturn

Be sure to proofread your work.

Matthew's science report has nine mistakes. Use proofreading marks to correct his work. Then rewrite the report. Add at least two describing words to the report.

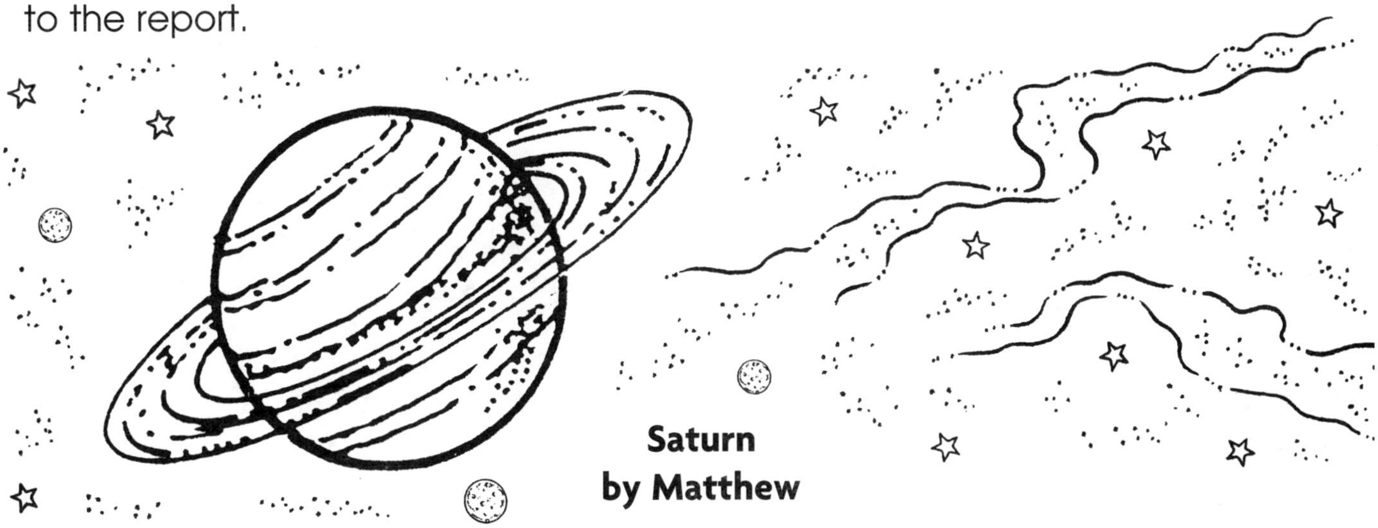

Saturn
by Matthew

Saturn is famous for the rings that surround it? its rings are made of ice, rock and dirt. The rings circle around the planet! Saturn is made of gas? saturn's gases are lighter than water That means Saturn would float if you put it into a tub of water Saturn has at least 17 moons

____

____

____

____

____

On another sheet of paper, write a short report about your favorite planet. Be sure to proofread it when you are done.

Banana-Rama

Color the word that is missing from each sentence.

1. We ______________ a spelling test yesterday. taked took
2. There ______________ frost on the ground. was were
3. Tommy ______________ the Statue of Liberty. seen saw
4. How ______________ elephants are at the zoo? much many
5. Claire ______________ her lizard to school. brought brang
6. Have you ______________ my dog? seen saw
7. Alyssa ______________ a new pair of skates. gots has
8. You ______________ supposed to finish your work. are is
9. We ______________ standing near a snake! were was
10. They ______________ a pig in the mud. seen saw
11. We ______________ our winter boots. wore weared
12. Is she ______________ to come over? gonna going
13. ______________ your cat climb trees? Do Does
14. Rosie ______________ cookies to the bake sale. brang brought

Name ____

An Apple a Day

Find the word that is incorrect in each sentence. Draw an apple around it and write the correct word on the line.

1. Laura brang a snack to camp. ____________________

2. I seen the sea lion show at the zoo. ____________________

3. Drew gots a dinosaur collection. ____________________

4. Mara taked her dog for a walk. ____________________

5. We is going to see the movie. ____________________

6. Jason runned to the playground. ____________________

7. How many pennies do you got? ____________________

8. The kids was having fun. ____________________

9. Did you saw the soccer game? ____________________

10. How much do that cost? ____________________

11. Kelly brang her cat to school! ____________________

12. I does my homework after school. ____________________

Eat an apple. Then on another sheet of paper, write a statement, a question, and an exclamation describing the apple. Be sure each sentence uses correct words.

Name ______________________

Stories of Nature

Sentences should be written in the correct order to tell a story.

Finish the stories by writing a sentence about each of the last two pictures.

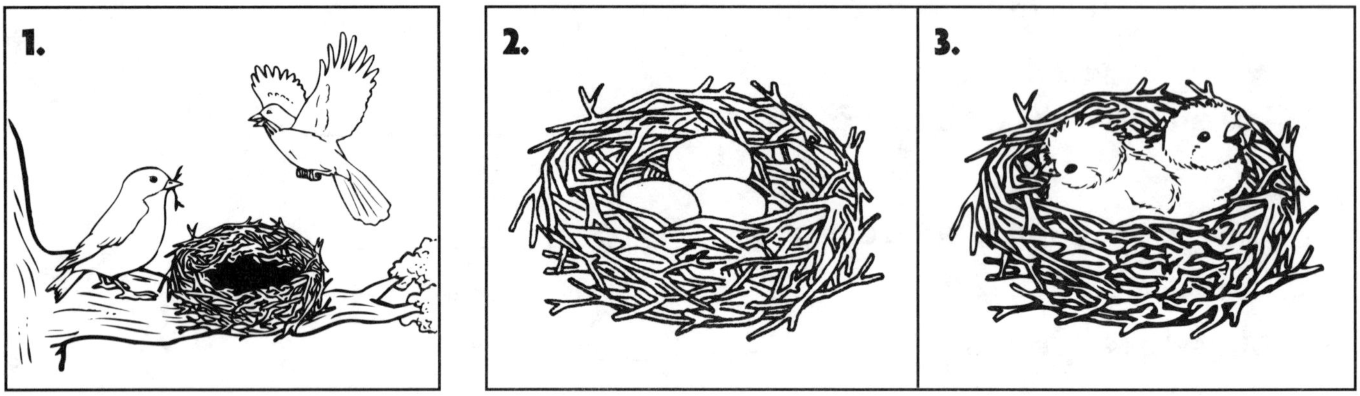

First: Two birds build a nest.

Next: ______________________

Last: ______________________

First: A flower bud grows.

Next: ______________________

Last: ______________________

Name ________________________________

Nestled in a Nest

Write a sentence about each picture to make your own story.

____
____
____

____
____
____

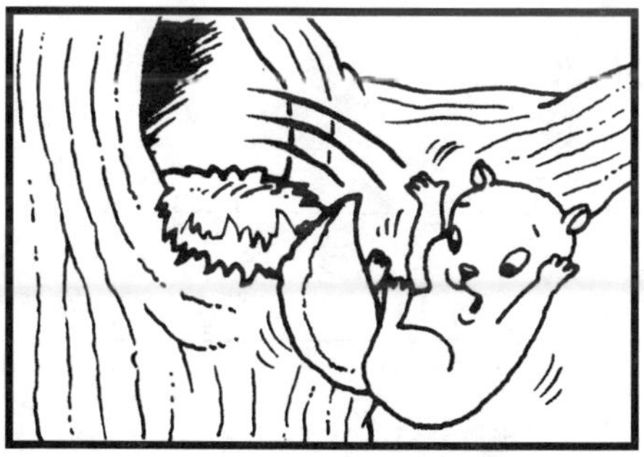

____
____
____

____
____
____

Read your story to a friend.

Name ______________________________

Writing the middle and end of stories

Stories on Parade

Stories have a **beginning** *(B), a* **middle** *(M), and an* **end** *(E).*

Write a middle sentence that tells what happens next. Then write an ending sentence that tells what happens last.

B **During the parade, five funny clowns jumped out of a purple bus.**

M **Next,** ______________________________

E **Finally,** ______________________________

B **A big balloon got loose in the wind.**

M **Next,** ______________________________

E **Finally,** ______________________________

B **A group of horses stopped right in front of us.**

M **Next,** ______________________________

E **Finally,** ______________________________

B **Some clowns were riding motorcycles.**

M **Next,** ______________________________

E **Finally,** ______________________________

On another sheet of paper, draw a picture of a parade that shows what is happening in the stories you wrote.

Name ______________________________

An Original Story

Choose a story idea from the list. Then write a beginning, middle, and ending sentence to make a story of your own. Color a picture to match each part.

The Best Birthday Ever | **King for a Day**

My Dog's Dream | **The Magic Rock**

B

First: ______________________________

____

____

____

M

Next: ______________________________

____

____

____

E

Last: ______________________________

____

____

____

Staple three sheets of paper together to make a book. Write another story and draw a picture for each part.

Name ____________________________

Once Upon a Time

*The **setting** of a story tells when or where it is happening.*

Imagine that you are writing a story for each picture below. How will you describe the setting? Write a sentence describing each setting.

setting	→	characters	→	problem	→	solution

It was a hot morning in the desert.

On another sheet of paper, describe the setting of your favorite movie.

Name ____________________

All Kinds of Characters

The people or animals in a story are called **characters.**

Some characters are likable and others are not. Write a describing sentence about each character. Be sure to give each character a name.

setting → **characters** → **problem** → **solution**

____

____

____

____

____

____

____

____

____

On another sheet of paper, make a list of four people you know well. Write three words that describe each of them. Cross out the four names and write animal names instead. Now you have four characters to use in your next story!

Name ______________________________

That's a Problem!

To make a story exciting, one of the characters often runs into a **problem.**

Think about each character in the sentences below. What could happen that would make a problem for that character? Write the next sentence creating a problem.

setting → **characters** → **problem** → **solution**

1. Beauty Butterfly was enjoying the warm spring day.

____

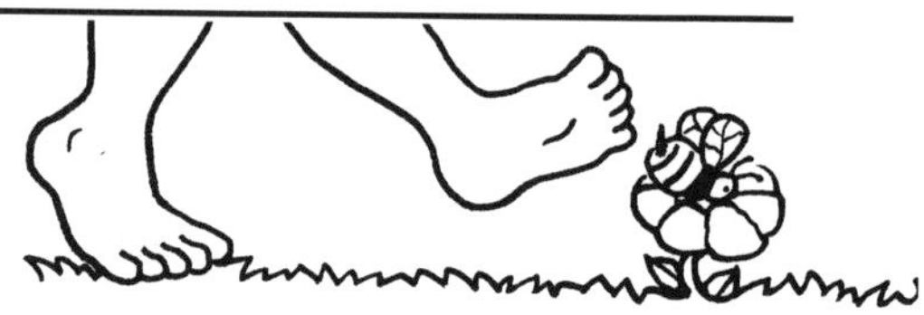

2. Jesse was supposed to wear shoes outside.

____

3. Gabby could not wait to bite into her apple.

____

4. Ben smacked the baseball into the air.

____

5. Barney Bass had never seen such a big worm!

____

Good Solution!

At the end of a story, the problem is usually solved. This is called the **solution**.

Read the beginning and middle parts of the stories below. Write an ending solution for each.

setting → **characters** → **problem** → **solution**

David and his dog, Spot, were best friends. They went everywhere together. At bedtime, David whistled for Spot to jump in his bed. One winter night, David whistled and whistled, but Spot did not come.

____

____

____

Josh loved second grade, but he did not like recess. Josh's class was always the last one out to the playground. Every day, Josh ran to get a swing, but they were always taken.

____

____

____

On another sheet of paper, make a list of three problems you have faced. How did you solve each problem?

Name ____________________

The Mighty Knight

*A **story map** helps you plan the setting, characters, problem, and solution.*

Write a sentence about each part of the map to make a story.

____

____

____

____

____

____

____

____

____

____

Read your story to a friend.

Name ______________________________

A Story Fit for a King

Use a story map to help plan your story before you begin writing.

Complete the map. Then use it to write a story "fit for a king."

	→		→		→	

____

____

____

____

____

____

____

____

____

____

Turn your story into a puppet show! Perform your puppet show for someone at home.

Name ____ **Proofreading**

The Father of Our Country

After you finish writing, go back and look for mistakes.

Use the proofreading marks to correct eight mistakes in the letter.

m̲̲ars **= Make a capital letter.** (?) **= Add a question mark.** (!) **= Add an exclamation point.**

(.) **= Add a period.** (,) **= Add a comma.**

Dear Friend,

my job as the first president of the United States was hard My friends and I had to make new laws new money, and new jobs. the capital was in New York when I became president. then it moved to Philadelphia. Is the capital still there. Who is the president today! I would love to see how the U.S. has changed over the past two hundred years?

Sincerely,

George Washington

On another sheet of paper, write a letter to today's president. The White House address is: 1600 Pennsylvania Avenue Washington, D.C. 20500.

Presidential Pen Pals

*A **friendly letter** has five parts: the date, greeting, body, closing, and signature.*

Use the five parts to write a letter back to George Washington. Be sure to proofread your work for mistakes.

____
(today's date)

______________________,
(greeting)

____
(body)

____

____

____

____

____

____

____

____

______________________,
(closing)

____
(your name)

Page 4
Many of; Our teacher; The reading; The globe; We study; Our class

Page 5
1. Art class; 2. Today we; 3. First, we; 4. The next; 5. My teacher; 6. Next week

Page 6
1. The blue whale is the largest animal in the world. 2. Even dinosaurs were not as large as the blue whale. 3. Blue whales are not part of the fish family. 4. The blue whale has no teeth. 5. Blue whales eat tiny sea creatures. 6. Blue whales have two blowholes.

Page 7
Sentences will vary.

Page 8
1. Where is the king's castle? 2. Who helped Humpty Dumpty? 3. Why did the cow jump over the moon? 4. Will the frog become a prince? 5. Could the three mice see?

Page 9
Sentences will vary.

Page 10
1. .; 2. ?; 3. ?; 4. .; 5. ?; 6. .; 7. ?; 8. .

Page 11
1. The sun is the closest star to Earth. 2. The sun is not the brightest star. 3. What is the temperature of the sun? 4. The sun is a ball of hot gas. 5. How large is the sun? 6. Will the sun ever burn out?

Page 12
Sentences will vary.

Page 13
Dear Mom and Dad,
Camp is so cool! Today we went swimming. Do you know what the best part of camp is? I think fishing is my favorite thing to do. Did you feed my hamster? I really miss you.
Love, Dalton

Sentences will vary.

Page 14
1. .; 2. ?; 3. !; 4. ?; 5. .; 6. !; 7. ?; 8. .; 9. ?; 10. !; 11. .; 12. ?

Page 15
Sentences will vary.

Page 16
Sentences will vary.

Page 17
Sentences will vary.

Page 18
Sentences may vary. Possible answers: 1. A boy climbs a tree in his backyard. 2. A cat plays with fish in the living room. 3. A bunny eats a carrot in the garden.

Page 19
Sentences and pictures will vary.

Page 20
Lists of words will vary.

Page 21
Answers will vary. 1. fat, three; 2. wooden, cold; 3. Orange, sunny; 4. lazy, muddy; 5. thirsty, shallow; 6. funny, black

Page 22
Describing words will vary.

Page 23
Sentences will vary.

Page 24
Sentences will vary.

Page 25
Sentences will vary.

Page 26
1. The party was fun and exciting. 2. We blew up orange and red balloons. 3. We ate cake and ice cream. 4. The cake frosting was green and yellow. 5. We made a bookmark and a clay pot. 6. We brought games and prizes.

Page 27
1. These peanuts and pretzels are salty. 2. The first graders and second graders eat lunch at noon. 3. Where is the salt and pepper? 4. The napkins and forks are on the table. 5. Are the muffins and cookies in the oven? 6. Michael and Stephen bought lunch today.

Page 28
1. Fill a cup with water and add some flower seeds. 2. This will soften the seeds because they are hard. 3. Fill a cup with dirt while the seeds soak in water. 4. Bury the seeds in the cup until the dirt covers them. 5. Add water to the plant but do not add too much. 6. Set the cup in the sun so the plant will grow.

Page 29
Sentences will vary.

Page 30
Sentences will vary.

Page 31
Sentences will vary.

Page 32
Describing words will vary. 1. Sometimes I can see Mars, Jupiter, and Saturn with my telescope. 2. There are many stars in our galaxy. 3. Comets are large pieces of ice and rock. 4. The sun is really a huge star. 5. Is there life on any other planet? 6. Look at that beautiful shooting star! 7. Can you imagine traveling in space? 8. I think I saw a little alien.

Page 33
Describing words will vary.

Saturn is famous for the rings that surround it. Its rings are made of ice, rock, and dirt. The rings circle around the planet. Saturn is made of gas. Saturn's gases are lighter than water. That means Saturn would float if you put it into a tub of water. Saturn has a least 17 moons.

Page 34
1. took; 2. was; 3. saw; 4. many; 5. brought; 6. seen; 7. has; 8. are; 9. were; 10. saw; 11. wore; 12. going; 13. Does; 14. brought

Page 35
1. ~~brang~~, brought; 2. ~~seen~~, saw; 3. ~~gots~~, has; 4. ~~taked~~, took; 5. ~~is~~, are; 6. ~~runned~~, ran; 7. ~~got~~, have; 8. ~~was~~, were; 9. ~~saw~~, see; 10. ~~do~~, does; 11. ~~brang~~, brought; 12. ~~does~~, do

Page 36
Sentences will vary.

Page 37
Sentences will vary.

Page 38
Sentences will vary.

Page 39
Stories will vary.

Page 40
Sentences will vary.

Page 41
Sentences will vary.

Page 42
Sentences will vary.

Page 43
Answers will vary.

Page 44
Stories will vary.

Page 45
Stories will vary.

Page 46
Dear Friend,
My job as the first president of the United States was hard. My friends and I had to make new laws, new money, and new jobs. The capital was in New York when I became president. Then it moved to Philadelphia. Is the capital still there? Who is the president today? I would love to see how the U.S. has changed over the past two hundred years!
Sincerely,
George Washington

Page 47
Letters will vary.